No Whistling on a Sunday

An Oral History of the Stockbridge Colonies

Contents

PRODUCED BY THE COLONIES ORAL HISTORY GROUP

Published by Lomond Books

Introduction

The story behind the building of the Colonies has already been told in *The Colonies of Stockbridge* which was first published in 1984 and re-issued in 1998. *No Whistling on a Sunday* is the story of the people of the Colonies, told by the people and illustrated with their own photographs. It was first published in 1993, and apart from a few new photographs and a different format, the content of this 1999 edition is the same as the original.

The project which led to this book began in 1991 when several Colonies residents met together to form an oral history group. The task they set themselves was to interview a selection of those residents who had lived in the Colonies for all or most of their lives and whose memories of the area went back 60 years or more.

This picture was taken at Reid Terrace in the summer of 1992. It shows some of the people who took part in the Colonies oral history project. From top left they are: Alison Neilson-Dow (interviewer), Gordon McNeilage, Anna Duncan, Mary MacNamara, Eddie Kinnaird, George Goodall, Bertha Davidson, Nan Macdonald, Elsie Crawford, Rachel Valentine, Helen Jennings, Irene Paterson, Ewan Hogg, Jocky Hogg, Anne Fortune (interviewer).

Twenty-three residents were interviewed and it is extracts from their conversations that make up this book. Their names are listed below:

Mary Allan	Anna Duncan	Mary MacNamara
Joyce Anderson	Evelyn Flint	Gordon McNeilage
Anne Armstrong	John Flint	Peggy Ormiston
Isabella Barclay	George Goodall	Irene Paterson
Kate Buchanan	Jocky Hogg	Margaret Skinner
Elsie Crawford	Helen Jennings	Stan Suttie
Chrissie Cutt	Eddie Kinnaird	Rachel Valentine
Bertha Davidson	Nan Macdonald	

The memories of those who were interviewed stretch back to the years when the last houses were being built. This was a time when families were usually large but means were modest; when marbles, peevers and street games were the stuff of entertainment; when houses and streets were lit by gas and when customs and rituals were strictly observed – there was 'no whistling on a Sunday' and no washing either!

This 'people's story' is a unique social document of an unusual community which, despite many changes in recent years, is still very much a community, greatly enriched by the presence of those – and more – whose memories this book enables us to share.

Rose Pipes (Editor)

Acknowledgements

Interviews were conducted by: Alan Cameron, Jenia Collingwood, Anne Fortune, Judy Fowlie, Mary MacLeod, Alice Maxwell, Alison Neilson-Dow, Rose Pipes.

We are grateful to the following for their help in the production of this book: The Scotsman Publications Ltd for permission to reproduce the photograph on page 20; Eddy Fawdry for taking the photographs on page 2, 9 and 17; Liz Robertson for the original cover design; and all those Colonies residents who supplied photographs.

ISBN 0 947782 04 4

First edition: 1993; Revised edition: 1999
Revised edition published by Lomond Books, Edinburgh

Layout by The Graphics Company, Edinburgh.
Printed and bound by Bell & Bain Ltd.
Typeset in Adobe Garamond.

Living in the Colonies

"There are still quite a lot living here that I knew when I was young. Not many, but there are. People changed houses a lot. Quite a lot moved away to Comely Bank, but a lot of them came back to the Colonies. And the same with people where their parents moved away, they came back to the Colonies. I think they must have just had a happy childhood here; happy memories of the place. Plus it was quite a nice place to bring up children. There was no traffic long ago and you could play in the street without bother at all. You'd go to the school, your mother might meet you in the afternoon, but she didn't have to take you back and forward the way they do now. Of course, there was always a crowd of you going, but there was none of this carry on. You didn't really know many people at the other end of the Colonies, you sort of kept to your own end. We always talked about 'the other end'. It's not so towny. Long ago it was like a village. You were sort of separated. You talked about going up to the town and down to Leith. I mean it was quite a novelty to go up the town."

"Somebody who lived in Saunders Street said they thought people living in the Colonies were a lot of snobs. Oh aye, kind of fancied themselves. But on the whole they weren't bad people. They were a lot of decent working class people who had high standards for themselves... for their children as well, and they expected a lot of proper behaviour. The children were expected to do well. I liked living in the Colonies. It was a homely place to be and you knew people. I knew a lot of people to speak to, not necessarily as friends. We didn't visit each other's houses. People didn't do things together – everybody lived their own life. There was a wee bit of people trying to be better than others, some people were definitely up and coming – like any community really."

"It was a right wee community down here. People looked after each other. You always had a good neighbour. The parents didn't go into each other's houses, the children did. The adults were that little bit reserved. We had a happy time. It was a good place to be a child in. We didn't have the traffic we have now, and you could play out in the street. We had very little, materially. Some people were a bit snooty. Not so much down here, they were all in the same category – all working – and they didn't envy what others could get. But in the church, that was one thing you did find – 'see so and so – see how she's dressed'. They were inclined to look down on somebody who was poor-looking coming in."

"I love it here. I really love it. They'll carry me out. I've got a quiet place, in the corner; I can sit in my garden in the summer time. It used to be like a village and everybody knew everybody else and they had time to talk. They'd sit out and have cups of tea and have wee picnics for the kids. That was when I was young. People's houses were more private – they helped each other but they didn't go in and out of each other's houses. You called your neighbours 'Auntie'. If there was a funeral you pulled the blinds down – it was respect. The children were brought in."

"It was different in those days, there was a real caring atmosphere. People were interested in one another and helped each other. Now, apart from a few in my street, I don't know anybody. We could go out to the shops and just pull the door to, and even leave it open in the summer, and there was no glass middle door then. Now I wouldn't move from here across to the other side without putting on the safety catch."

"In the Colonies you are your own boss and your garden ... when it's your own garden you appreciate it very much more. My friend lived at Comely Bank and the kids couldn't play because of the washing being out. Our kids had freedom – they were safe in the street."

Children in Collins/Balmoral. Taken around 1902.

"It was a very close-knit, friendly community. There used to be a friendly rivalry and we used to call it 'our own half of the Colonies' and the 'other half' was always the other end. You never referred to it as anything else but the 'other end'. So, of course, when I moved to it, it was bad! My mother and father stayed in Rossie Place and they used to walk down this way when my brother and I were babies. My mother always said that she'd love to live here. Again, the community spirit, and people were very friendly. There's not many places that have the river and the trees. Both parents coming from the country thought it was the nearest thing they'd get to their old life, and that probably has to do with it too.

There are many more professional people in the Colonies than before. But I would still say that it has the community spirit. The shops have gone apart from one. When the shops were here, it was nice because that was quite a meeting place for neighbours you know. It's changed a bit. So many houses have been built out – when the houses were originally built there were no attics at all in many of them."

"The neighbours all used to know each other. I don't know who stays in the first house here – no idea. Everything was more neighbourly and my mother, when we were young was the one, when anything went wrong, she was the person that you came for. She would go and do whatever, advise or whatever. So we were brought up that if there's anything you can do for anybody, it's your duty to do it – get on with it. And I think all the families were brought up in the same way. That's changing. And of course people are busier now, they're out working, the wife, the mother, too. There's not the same time. There's no time for neighbourliness. The mothers are out working and when they come back they've the shopping and the house to do – they've no time to see what's going on next door.

People got to know each other in the street when they were hanging out the washing. These stairs were brushed down every day, washed down every week, and I suppose they'd be chatting while they were doing that. You'd maybe go in for a chat but you wouldn't be invited for tea or for a meal I don't think. It was much more informal."

"I always fancied staying down the Colonies. It probably stemmed from the time when I delivered papers here. I always fancied them. My wife always fancied them. I don't know why we liked them. It is handy for transport – no distance to anywhere. Also, rates were low. I once said to my wife when they were putting up the Barratt houses 'Would you like to go along there?' 'Not on your life, I like my ain wee hoose'. And I tell you, my son had a Barratt house in Bo'ness and he only lasted a year. To be honest, it was rubbish. Oh no, I prefer a solid house. This house was built in 1872."

"I like living here because it's central. It's easy to get to town. There's a lot here and it's quiet and people help me with my shopping because I can't get out. I wouldn't move from here."

"There were big families all around. There were five girls next door – the Wilson's – there were nine of them ... the Thomsons across the road – there were five of them and four of the Lyalls. It was a tight community.

You were always there if you were needed. You weren't always in and out of one another's houses like now. Most people had their main meal at lunch-time so people were around a lot more. You'd go and speak to people on their steps. We had an allotment. A lot of people did. We'd go up there in an evening. It's not the same here now. People aren't as friendly. They go off to work in their cars and come back in the evenings and disappear into their houses. You used to see more of people. If you went up to the Store you sat on a form and got talking to everyone."

"When I was at school you used to get your photo taken. And they'd say 'How many of you are there?' And I'd say 'six of us.' So they'd say 'Right. Go and collect them'." (Quote from Bertha Davidson, seated in the centre of the picture, surrounded by her brothers and sisters.)

"The Colonies are a nice place to stay. They are central – it's easy to get into the town. Up until recently it's been quiet traffic-wise. It felt neighbourly. For years there were very very few changes in this street. They seemed to be the same people. Then of course occasionally somebody died, or moved away. Recently a lot of new people have been coming into the streets. I don't know half of them yet in this street. Generally, people did get on. Our two children seem quite happy living here. They never make any complaints about it anyway! Even when they were young traffic wasn't too bad."

"Och, you knew everybody then. There were children in nearly every house. We didn't have neighbours in much. The next-door neighbours – they were all very friendly. And sometimes weeks would pass and we wouldn't see them. It was only if there was trouble she was in, you know, to help. We always got on well with everyone. My mother always said there was only one woman in her life she quarrelled with when she lived in Teviotdale. They had outside stairs and they used to take turns to clean it. This woman used to object to my brother's chums coming up the stair."

"It was a neighbourly place to live. You never had to lock up. You could go along to the shops and not bother yourself. The only conflicts were if you were playing ball, playing rounders or that, if it went in some of the gardens that were fussy. My mother always used to say, 'If anyone gives you a row, don't give them cheek!' I can't remember anyone we were against. We were all much the same – there was nobody who seemed to be better off. If there were only two in a family they were better off, but they nearly all had families. I left the Colonies when I married, and when I came back I hated it. We'd had a nice new house with everything. I don't know why I hated coming back here. The fires for one thing. We used to have to bring up coal from the cellar because we always liked a nice fire. But when we got all the things done... I like it now. I wouldn't like to move – but mind you, there might be some day when I'll have to move if I find the stair too much. But you feel that it's still the same. I know a lot of people here."

Accommodation

"In the wee bedroom there was a double bed and the two girls slept in it and Faither (my husband) and I slept in the kitchen. In the front room there was a big bed and the two boys slept in that. When Finlay was ill he had to get a bed to himself, so it was two three-quarter beds went into the front room then. Sometimes, to stop the nonsense, the girls were put in with the boys and sometimes they just slept anywhere that suited.

In the kitchen there was a Triplex grate. I cooked on that and I had the flues cleaned every Friday morning otherwise I couldn't get any heat in the oven. We had gas light – no electricity or hot water. I offered to pay for it – to pay half with the landlord – I was willing to pay my share. He said that if I wanted the luxury of electric light I could pay for it myself. Later on I had a gas ring attached to a tap and the ring sat on the fire hearth. That did for boiling the kettle in the morning. There was always a big hassle about breaking the gas mantles in the lights. If you put the match too near it, you broke the damn thing. The house was often dark because you didn't light the gas in the lobby because it was a fire risk – it was just above the toilet

door and the same in the wee bedroom. It wasn't worth the risk of fire. One night I had put it on fairly low, and for some reason Faither must have turned it up and, or course, it burned all the paint. We could have had a fire that time – sometimes he could be so stupid!

There was a toilet in the middle of the house, the size of a cupboard. Just a toilet, no washbasin. The door faced you as you came in the front door and there was no light in that. The gas light above the door was supposed to light it. There was a window above the door but it was always dark. Late on we improvised a wee torch battery and a bulb which we used occasionally. Then there was the 'glory hole' next to the toilet – a big cupboard – and that's where we had to go when the sirens went. It was our air raid shelter.

9

In the front room we had two beds, a settee, a wardrobe, a chest of drawers and a writing bureau. In the kitchen there was a double bed in the recess, two chairs on either side of the fire, a table and wooden chairs and a small sideboard at the back of the table. There was a stone sink and tub in the window with brass taps that used to go green with verdigris if you forgot to clean them. In the wee bedroom there was just room for a small bed, a wardrobe and a chair between them.

I used to store the coal in the coal bunker in the garden and under the floor. We had quite a deep cellar under the house, about four feet deep. It went right under the house and it was awfy dark but you could see the grating at the other end of the house. That's why you never got any dry rot in the house – it was always dry. There was a trap door in front of the sink in the kitchen and Faither was aye pottering about in the cellar and leaving the trap door open. Anne fell down it one day and had concussion. The heating was just by one fire, no fire in the wee bedroom, and the fire in the front room – that was only lit once in a while. It was a lot of work. That was a marble fireplace."

"When Alistair was a baby he was in the cot in with us in the big room (the parlour) and Ian was in the wee bedroom. When Helena came she was in the cot and Alistair shared with Ian in the wee room. When she was older I'd made the big bedroom into a sitting room with a put-you-up in the kitchen. We had a recess in the kitchen but I made that into a cupboard because part of the bathroom was in that recess and we included the cupboard beside the fire into it. We are the newer houses (Dunrobin Place) so we have the toilets at the front door. When we were putting in the bathroom Ali said 'Where are we going to put all that stuff out of the cubby hole?' And I said 'I'll find somewhere for it!'; I was dying to have a bathroom."

"My parents slept in the kitchen in the recess. When we were small Bob and I both slept in a bed in the wee bedroom. When we got bigger Bob slept in a bed in the parlour. The small bedroom had a bed, a dressing table and a sewing machine. The kitchen had a bunker in the window and a range where my mother cooked. On the right side of the range there was a press. There was a trap door to the cellar in front of the sink where we kept coal and there was a grandfather clock on the left side of the fireplace. We had gas light and sometimes paraffin lamps.

The bed was in the recess with linen sheets and blankets and with a kind of woven cover on it with tassels; two fireside chairs; a kitchen table in the middle of the room with chairs round it. There was lino on the floor and a hooked rag rug in front of the fire. It was made by hooking fabric scraps through a piece of sacking. My mother made these and we had to help her. There was a pulley for washing in the kitchen. The range had to be black leaded. I usually did that after my mother died – spit and polish, as they say. There was a high shelf round the room for the best dishes. On the mantelpiece there were candlesticks. There were no pictures, I think we didn't go in much for pictures. We didn't have curtains, maybe lace ones or a blind with lace on it. In the lobby there was the 'dark closet' – a cupboard where there was a kist with sheets and blankets my mother got for wedding presents and other things – a storage place. Then there was the toilet in the middle of the house with the gas light above the door. Linoleum on the floors and varnished paper on the walls.

The parlour had a sideboard, I mind that – all my mother's best dishes in that – and a settee and two chairs in there, and a white marble fireplace. The fire was only lit on high days and holidays, or if we had visitors. When Bob got older there was a bed in there too, and the gas light in the middle of the room. Lino in there too, and lace curtains. The rooms were all wallpaper except the lobby which was varnished."

"We had a bath in the walk-in cupboard (upstairs) and it was just cold water, and the toilet was under the stairs. We've kept it because of George's leg, going up and down that stair. We took a big bit off the bedroom, because it was colossal. There was a wash-hand basin in the bedroom, when we came, because there was a dentist and he had rented it and he pulled all the teeth up the stair. So he used the room upstairs as a surgery and used cold water in the basin."

"You went up the stair – it was an internal stair (Glenogle Terrace) – there was a small landing. The toilet was on your left, just enough room to get in and no more. Next to that was what we called the 'lobby press'. Next to that was the back bedroom off it. He divided what was the small bedroom at the front and opened a door up at the top of the stair and made a bathroom and kitchenette. So we had a livingroom and two wee rooms. At first my sister Connie and I were in that wee bedroom at the front and then she put a settee in the other room and slept there and we went to the back room. Later on we took my grandmother in. We had her for ten years. My mother slept with her because she had to keep an eye on her. It was a squeeze, but, of course, we sere sent away in 1939 when Frank was only a baby. We were evacuated to Craigellachie in Banffshire."

"I slept in the wee room off the kitchen There were five brothers in the one bed. The girls slept in the big room and my father and mother in the kitchen. The range is still there, in the kitchen. My mother cooked on that, and we had paraffin oil lamps that sat in the middle of the table. No gas or electricity for years (Reid Terrace).

We made our own carpets out of old cloth. My mother cut it up to make them. We had a sort of wax cloth on the floor. There was one big table and a horsehair couch. There were shelves on the walls with ornaments. We had those big copper pots and pans and bowls and plates right along the wall. There was a bed in the recess with homemade blankets. My mother made them herself. We used to wash ourselves in the sink at the window.

We had lace curtains. I set fire to them with the candle once! There was no wallpaper. The walls were painted red and green. I remember, half and half. Top half red and the bottom green. That was on for years. We had a cellar all the way along under the houses, not just ours. I mind we used to have rats in the cellar. When you lifted the trap door you'd see them running about underneath. I think they came after they knocked the houses and shops down in Deanhaugh Street. They never touched you though."

"I was born in number 1 Rintoul in the wee room with a wee window. There was a cellar in the floor that my mother had to take up the lid to lift and put the coal in and my brother was nearly killed. He opened the lid and then she went to tell the coalman to come and they were shutting the lid when she heard him say 'Don't shut the lid, I'm here'. He'd been under there.

We didn't have a bath to begin with and we didn't even have a sink, it was a jaw box. It's like a kitchen cupboard. It's just a press really. The front room had a good fire. Mother had the fireplace tiled because they used to have a thing along the mantelpiece with tassels on it. It was about 12 feet long with wee tassels and if the wind was blowing the wrong way the smoke – and upstairs too was terrible – short chimney – the wind just blew it into the room. It was made of serge and was crimson. This was to be posh. It was about 12 inches deep but it must have been for the smoke too. Most folk had them."

"We started at 17 Bell Place. There were six children. We had a wash house in the garden, down by the river. It was the only one that was in the Colonies I think. Our house had an attic, yes, but the house next door didn't. There was only the two rooms next door. No, we had the two rooms upstairs. It was very funny, because the water for the sink was in the well of the stair. It will be different now because these young people come in and do all sorts. The toilet was right opposite the door.

My younger sister and I were with my parents, this is probably why we moved you see, and my brothers were in the other room upstairs, and the sisters had the bed in the sitting room. A lot of people had their bed in the living room, but ours was in the sitting room which we used quite a lot. The kitchen was only in the well of the stair, it was only the water and the sink, and cupboards and something under the stair for pots and things, I think, no it was just in the ... and the stair went up and it was just a very small place."

"Most of the houses didn't have big windows upstairs. Just skylights and coomed ceilings. A few didn't have stairs going up. They had toilets, then the people that built out upstairs put bathrooms in. That would have been round about the 50s. There's someone along there who still doesn't have a bathroom. They still have a plunge bath once a week at the Baths."

The Johnston family outside their house at No. 8 Rintoul Place. Taken in 1940.

"My father's brother was a bachelor and lived with his mother. During the First World War she died and when he came back from the war he came to live with us. My two sisters had the small bedroom upstairs, my brother and uncle had the big bedroom upstairs and I had the small bedroom off the kitchen and my parents slept in the kitchen. We still had the front room – that was the front room! It was kept clean and tidy. I remember a beautiful red kind of velvet cultured paper. We had a white marble fireplace.

We didn't have a bath when we went first, but we had what we called 'the howff', that was built out into a bathroom. The toilet was under the stairs. Our heating was by coal fires, there were coal fires upstairs in the two bedrooms and two fires downstairs, in the front room and the kitchen.

Years later, the little bedroom was made into a scullery and the kitchen was modernised and made into a living room. The coal bunker was taken away that was in the window – and the big range was taken away. It had a big oven and hot water. You had to draw water off from a tap. You'd collect your hot water and take it over to the sink. The sink was in a horrible place behind a door. When we got the scullery it was moved in there. Originally though, when you came in one door the other door was right behind it and it was always awkward. It was in a sort of cupboard. My mother cooked on the range and the oven was there. We had gas lighting and 'bypasses', which meant that when you went in, you just pulled the wee cord and the light came on. We didn't need matches for the living room and the lobby. The light was hanging from the middle of the lobby ceiling and you just pulled the chain."

"Eight of us lived in a low door with no hot water. Three boys in the wee room off the kitchen, three girls in the front room and my mother and father in the bed recess. When we were young, three were in the one bed. That was quite common. The front room had a settee, and plush stuff. Two arm chairs – and my mother kept it locked so we couldn't go and play in there."

"There were eight children, four of each. When we came to Bell Place there were seven of us. My oldest sister and my youngest sister (who died when she was 14) in the small bedroom off the living room. Nellie and I – the next two – we slept in the small room upstairs with the skylight window. There was two double beds in the big bedroom and Burt slept in one and the other two boys slept in the other bed. Mother and Dad slept in the living room/kitchen. They had just a double bed – they had a job getting in for the size. After the family was married and that, Dad was ill and came home from hospital and Mother put a bed up in the sitting room and he said 'There's to be no bed in there, we must keep a sitting room.' He said 'I'm not sleeping in that room'. So she had to get the bed shifted back into the living room. So he got that. Dad sat in the sitting room all the time reading. He loved to read – liked quietness. We had, not a range, but a big black fireplace. It was lovely because we had the ovens and we had the tank at the side for hot water and a brass tap."

Daily routines, food and cooking

"I got up at half-past five on a Friday to clean the flues, but otherwise at half-past six. I put the fire on and made the porridge. Nowadays I can make porridge in five minutes but then I had to have it boiled for 20 minutes. Faither use to be out in the summer at six o'clock and come home for his breakfast at nine. In the winter he started at nine. His hours were spread over the year. He usually finished at five. The children came home in the middle of the day too and had dinner. Then high tea in the afternoon. How I did it, I don't know. The kids out to school, then me out to work and home to make the dinner. It was hard going – no wonder I was aye runnin'.

We ate what we could afford. I used to bake in the oven. That was quite difficult, getting it to the right temperature. I used to make scones, rock buns, pancakes on the girdle. My rough puff pastry had a good reputation too. We ate soups, stovies, mince and potatoes, liver, stews. It had to be simple with the difficulty of cooking on the open fire or on one gas ring. You made the best of it."

A typical Colonies kitchen range.

"My mother cooked wonderful meals on an open fire. She was a wee bit better than my granny. She had a big black iron kettle – well polished – she was a right black-leader. It stood full all the time so there was always hot water that way. I always think stews tasted far better in the iron pots we had. My mother wasn't a baker but she was an awful good cook. She made what we called 'cravers' – a kind of pancake in the frying pan. They were lovely, you were just eating them as she make them – usually on Sunday. That was a sort of lunch – a cup of tea and a craver. Sometimes she did a girdle scone but she did those in a great big frying pan – a bit like a girdle. She didn't use the oven much except for rice pudding.

I didn't help her much in the house. She wouldn't have me. She'd say 'I cannae be bothered – that's my job through the day'. She was a worker and she loved her work. She'd say 'I hope I die cleaning the windaes'."

"My dad was on shift work so he'd be an early riser one week and a late the next. The tramcars and buses used to start about six in the morning so he'd be up at half-past four. We had porridge – cornflakes were a luxury. We went to school and came home for our dinner. We ate things like boiled beef, soup, pudding – simple food. We came home even from Flora's for our dinner. We had a high tea when we came home in the afternoon. My mother was a good cook. We were usually in bed by seven or eight. We had to do our homework before we got out to play. We changed out of our school clothes and into play clothes. Your school clothes had to do you as long as possible."

"My mother got up first, got the fire on and got my faither out to his work. Then we'd get up for the school. You'd have to get yourself cleaned. Cold water, nae hot water in those days. We had all homemade stuff – kale, treacle scones, pancakes, scotch broth. You thought you were awfy lucky if you got a nice bun. We ate as much bread as you'd want and the soup would last two days. She made these great treacle scones, we'd be standing at the door waiting for them. They were great. And girdle scones too, and tatties, plenty tatties and mince. She must have been quite a woman."

"We had mince and potatoes and semolina pudding. Oh, how I hated it – had to eat it. And Effel Tower pudding. It was like sago in the custard and you had to eat it. For the 14-18 War we had some horrible turnip and potatoes boiled – my mother called it rummetetump – it was just mixed up with a wee bit margarine and that was our main meal. They used to go up to the health shop in Hanover Street and get some kind of dates – it was chopped up instead of sugar, you see we had no sugar. The worst thing we had in the First War was Keiller's jam. It was gelatine with flavouring and colour in cardboard cartons. In the last war if the Store had any jam you just spread the word so that the place was besieged – everyone flying for it."

"My father always had bacon and egg. For us it was mostly porridge with bread and butter. I don't think we really had toast in those days. We had porridge summer and winter. My father carried what was called a piece and we had our main meal in the evening. There was always home-made soup of course, and stew or mince or fish, you know, to ring the changes. We had a lot of stew which was done with all the vegetables – turnips, carrots, onions – all mixed up in it. It also spread out the amount of meat there was too because things weren't easy then. It was quite difficult."

"The cooking was done on the fire, the range, in the living room. It was just a fire I think, oh, and a ring for boiling up a kettle, a gas ring, I think, but mostly on the fire. It's amazing isn't it? Oh, we always had a clootie dumpling for our birthdays! That was a special, for our birthdays, with threepennies and things in it. She used to do them during the war and send them to her brothers in France or wherever they were. Oh they were lovely. A lovely skin on them you know with the, you know, the cloth, the clootie, was covered in flour before it was rolled up in it and that makes a lovely shiny outer bit. If you got the threepenny bit, that was yours.

Helen and Bill Jennings in front of their Triplex grate which was used for cooking and heating water at 17 Kemp Place.

My father always had an allotment, and we'd plenty of vegetables, loads of vegetables. We always had porridge and big pots of soup. Potatoes, I don't know what we had with them. My mother used to make, I forget what you call it, like haggis, and onions...skirly. We used to have that and it was lovely. I don't remember so much about fruit. I think it was an occasion to have apples and oranges."

"My mother had to get us all up. We always had porridge for breakfast, then she'd light the fire. She had my grandmother to look after. There was a fire through in the other room but that was just lit on a Saturday and Sunday. Half-a-crown for a bag of coal. Then my mother would have lunch to prepare. It was the main meal of the day. On a Monday we had a corn beef hash because she was busy with the wash. My father would come back from work for lunch. On Sunday we always had a roast. In the evening we'd have fish or a boiled egg. When I was bringing the boys up we had dinner in the middle of the day. Most people had their main meal at lunch time so people were round a lot more."

"I was eight and went to school and never got home for lunch but I got a roll and a cup of cocoa for a penny from the school canteen. Mother was there all the time. Dad was on shifts on the Evening News. Sometimes he had to work late and sometimes early. Most places here had old-fashioned high tea about 6pm. We had everything but chicken because it was a very expensive luxury then. Meat was cheap. I never had chicken until I was semi-grown up. Mother used to make a lot of broth and buy a big bit of haugh that went in the broth. The haugh was used as the meat course. For pudding we had tapioca, semolina or custard. I went to bed between nine and ten."

"We had to get up and do the fires and take the carpets out and brush them out – no hoovers in those days. My father had to be at work at 8.30 – he left at the back of eight. I worked nine to six in the shop. There was never anything special to eat. Something that was special was a tin of fruit, maybe, for someone's birthday. I don't remember birthday cakes when I was young. We had clootie dumplings. They had silver threepennies or a sixpence inside."

"You came home from school. If you had homework to do you had to do it before you were allowed out. My father was on shifts. We came home about four. We had an evening meal about 5.30 – 6 o'clock. In summer time you were allowed to stay out a little later. I remember the soft balmy evenings – a lot of the ladies used to come out and sit out on the landings talking away. You don't see that much now. I don't know, the weather's not so nice now. When it was wet we played round the house – with books, or whatever."

"On a week day we all got up as late as possible and got dressed and you had your breakfast, your porridge, or whatever. We came back for lunch, home-made soup and potatoes and meat – sometimes the meat the soup was made of – and rice puddings and bread puddings. We always had plenty of food. We came home about three o'clock. You all had tea together before my father came in so that he could get peace, then he had his dinner. We had to do homework. The only time my father ever went out was a Saturday night. He used to get us all in because we wouldn't come in for our mother. We used to be terrified to go in for a drink. We used to say to our chums 'Oh you go, you'll not be kept in'. If we went near the door my father would say 'Time you were in'. Anyway, he used to go out on a Saturday and he used to get us all in and we were all supposed to be in our beds. And we used to watch for him going round the corner and we were all up and out playing and my mother used to say 'What if he comes back?' She was always terrified in case he came back. We used to keep half our clothes on underneath our night-dresses so we would get dressed quick and get back in again. He went to play cards with some men from Bruce Peebles."

"My mother would get up in the morning and clean out the range and light the fire. I think my father would start work about 8ish. He went away to his work and then we would get up and get washed and have our breakfast and usually you had to go messages before you went to school because there were no fridges or anything. There was a Store bakers, grocer, a butcher, so very often you had to go up there, to get the dinner for your mother to cook. And then you came home at lunch time from school. My father came home from his work and the soup would be on the table ready. He only had an hour and he had to get from up by the Theatre Royal. He came down on the tramcar to Canonmills and sometimes we'd be watching for him coming and we'd shout 'Oh, Mummy, here's Daddy coming', so his dinner was all ready for him. Then you'd go back to school again, then you came home and I used to go messages for an old lady in the next street. Then you were out to play. Then you had your tea when my father came home about half-past five or six – a high tea. You did have a proper lunch – soup, meat and maybe a milk pudding. High tea was maybe scrambled egg, bacon and egg. Not a lot, because as I say, they didn't have the money then that they have now."

"We came home for lunch and my father, when he was on night shift, would try one bed then another. And he'd say 'What's all this noise going on?' You can imagine six of us round the table. We used to say 'Don't make so much noise, you'll waken him'."

Washing clothes

"I went out to the wash-house, but when there were nappies to be done, you just steeped them in the tub and then I used to have a big pot thing that I put in the oven to heat the water. It was a big round zinc bath thing, I would put it in overnight and there was aye some hot water in the morning – not for tea, just for the washing. I went to the wash-house once a week, generally it was a Monday. I had an old pram and a zinc bath and I tied it on with ropes. One woman used to call me 'the wee woman with the big washing'! A lot of people from the Colonies used the wash-house. You got everything dried and mangled there. We also dried clothes on the pulley in the kitchen. One day the weight of washing on it broke the rope and it fell on Faither's head!"

The wash-house (steamie) at Henderson Row in 1976, the year it was closed.

"My mother had a tub and stand and a wringer and washboard. She kept it under the bed when she wasn't using it. Everything was kept under the beds. In No. 14 I washed at home too, but it was better, I had hot water from a back boiler on the range. It was connected to the tap at the sink. I had good hot water. My mother would wash in the sink and rinse in the tub. Monday was my washing day and we ironed in the afternoons if we got the washing dry, or on a Tuesday. We listened to the radio when we did the ironing. It was usually a story – that was lovely in No. 14.

I hated my mother's washing day – always on washing day it was fish and chips. When we were younger it was hot pies out of Ross the baker (where Preacher's is now). I got them when I came home from school. Sometimes we had stovies too. She said she had enough to do when she did the washing and could do without cooking too."

"My mother washed at a big wooden tub in the middle of the floor on a trestle and she had a great big iron pot that she carried from the fireplace. When she put the pot on it it covered the whole of the fireplace and that put the oven on and she baked while the clothes were boiling and then she had a scoop and took the water to the tub and washed them in the middle of the floor."

"By 1935, my mother still did the washing in the tub and she had a ringer. My mother – if she had a big washing like blankets – went up to the wash-house which was in Henderson Row. The booking there I'm not sure about, but you could get roughly speaking about 20 in because the dryers... you pulled them out of this wall and it was just all those poles along. It was like boilers, nothing that looked like a washing machine. We dried the clothes in the garden. You could dry them off better in the wash-house than you ever could do in the house so I think they were part-dried when you got them home. Monday was wash day. It was a ritual."

"We lived in 17 Bell Place, and an interesting thing about that was that the person obviously who owned our house must have owned the one at the bottom of Kemp, and that's why you'll maybe notice there's a door onto the path at the side of the water from there along to ours, up, and that was because they had the use of this wash-house that sits in the garden there. It was the only one that was in the Colonies I think. It's not in use now, but we as children used to get our baths down there. Two great big sinks you know, a great big boiler, fire underneath it, and after wash day, the fire would be lit in this boiler, and we used to get into these big sinks and have our bath. We had to go up steps to turn the tap. And there was a great big one of these old-fashioned mangles. The boiler did the washing and then the clothes were brought out into these two big sinks. Wash day was a lot of work, for six children to be washed for."

"The Store in Hamilton Place would take your wash – a bag wash was what they called it. It was two shillings, so you crammed as much into this bag as you could. You brought it back wet. My mother used to have a bag wash occasionally. It was a treat, otherwise she did it here. There was the wash-house in Henderson Row. I used to go there with blankets and things."

"The washing was done in the tub and there was a mangle. In Reid Terrace, of course, you could use your garden or use the front green but most people always used their garden. The green at that time was hardly ever used. It's always been a contention that if the low doors really wanted to push it, I think they could use it. We used the old flat iron for ironing. I had an older one I flung out recently where you lifted up a flap and you put in a shaped brick that you heated up to red hot in the fire."

"My mother had a Mrs Abbot and she came and took the washing along to the wash-house at Raeburn Place, near Dean Park Street. There was a wash-house there. It was near Bedford Street. She came every Monday with her steamie pram and took a basket of washing. I think it was 6d that she got for doing the wash. We had to hang it out and do the ironing and we went to Mrs Kinnear at 7 Balmoral Place to do the mangling. You went and did your own mangling. She was an old lady. We got all the sheets and pillowcases and folded them all at home. After drying them I was often sent over to do the mangling, sometimes my sister, it usually fell to me."

"We had hot water from the boiler thing. My mother had a mid-wife and she forgot to put the water in the boiler so it burst. So we didn't have the use of that. Mind you there were white sheets, petticoats, knickers – she did go to the steamie latterly and I used to take blankets and so on. The range was to heat water on and the sheets were put in a big boiler on it."

Using the Baths

"We used to have a zinc bath in front of the fire when the children were smaller. They got bathed in it. Then we went to the Baths – generally about once a week. You got it cheaper if you let them turn on the water – 3d, or 6d if you turned it on yourself. If you didn't have a bath in the house you used the Baths. But I didn't know a lot of people who used them. You'd see some old men going. Some people looked down on you if you went to the Baths – you were supposed to pretend you had a bath in the house."

Glenogle Baths and the gardens beside them where the Snakey path was later made.

"The boys used the Baths for swimming and for baths, and I did too. I used the gallery until I could afford a shilling one. To tell the truth I didn't really like the shilling ones because I had a lot of rather rotten things happen there. Folk who had been shaving themselves – and there were lumps of hair in the bath, that kind of thing. I stopped going because of things like that. It was better in the gallery. They turned the water on for you and if it was too hot it was terrible, you used to have to put your towel round you and get them to put more water in to make it cooler. I used the Baths when we were in Dunrobin before I was married. Tuesdays and Thursdays were women's days. If you were going out it was good to go and get a bath."

"We went swimming sometimes with the school. We got bathed in the house when we were wee. In fact, on the bank where the bridge is we used to go swimming underneath. When they used to clean out the Baths once a week and there was hot water coming out there, we used to get in the hot water – it's a fact! We used to swim out at the boxings, they were five feet deep. It was deep there, right from Balerno down to Leith. You could walk across now. It was deep then. I mind once a girl fell in and I had to get her out. A wee lassie was drowning. She was staying with her aunt in Reid Terrace. I came home from work one day and I saw all the folk at the railings and they were shouting that there was a wee lassie in the water and they were looking. I jumped over the railings, I don't know how I did it. I got her and held her up and my sister ran round to the other side on the Arboretum Avenue and helped me out with her. She had been hanging on the side of the boxings. I couldn't get her out myself, I don't know how I did it, I've only got one good leg!"

"They had a chute in the Baths and it was taken away because it was dangerous – folks were fleeing off! Ewan Hogg's brothers, they were great in the Baths. We used to have to go there for a bath. We didn't have a bath in the house so we went there for a plunge bath."

"I used to go to the Baths every day when I was younger – I must have been in Primary school. If you got there before four o'clock you got in for a penny. Four o'clock to five was a penny but after that it was 3d. You got longer though. Money being tight I used to run home and go into the four-five session and then the lady at the till sometimes asked me to get milk from Nellie the Dairy and if I did that I got in for nothing, so that was always a bonus."

"We put a shower in about 22 years ago. Before that we went to the Baths. It was about a shilling for a bath. They had baths on the first floor – big ones, in cubicles. Then upstairs were smaller baths and they ran the water for you, where downstairs you ran your own water, so you could take as much as you wanted. We went about twice a week."

"I used to go to the Baths about four times a week. It was a penny. But you didn't spend all morning there. There was an old bath attendant there. He must have been an ex-soldier, you know, he had one of these wee wax moustaches. He used to periodically ask to see your fingers. Well, if you'd been in the water a while they'd wrinkle and he, if he saw them wrinkled, would say 'OUT'. Oh, he was a real tartar. It was used then just as much as it is now because a penny was quite cheap, plus the fact you got a hot shower at the same time and a big hunk of carbolic soap for a wash.

They didn't have a chute but what they did have was rings and they were taken away as being too dangerous. The rope used to go along the whole length of the bath with rings from the ceiling and if you were very agile you could sort of get a tarzan-effect. They were about 10-12 feet up, but it was stopped. This was about the 1930s. They also had a couple of mats you could roll around on, but they were like these mats you clean your feet on, they were as jaggy as anything and you'd only a pair of togs on so it wasn't pleasant.

There were two types of bath in those days. You got a cheap one and a dearer one. The cheap one on one side – the attendant used to fill it up with water from a tap control on the outside. That was your lot – you went in and that was it finished, but if you paid a bit more you got taps in the inside so you could empty the bath and fill it up again. You got a towel and a bit of carbolic soap."

Church and Sundays

"We went to Saint Bernard's Davidson's in Henderson Row – it was Saint Bernard's South in those days. We took over the Davidson Church in Eyre Place. That was before the war. The children went to Sunday School there always. The main social activity for me was connected with the church. The Women's Guild, the Mother's Group, the Sunday School, the children's choir, the Boy's Brigade, the Girl's Guildry. On Sundays we went to church and I got up a bit later. I didn't make porridge on a Sunday. They got tea and toast. Then after church we had dinner – never anything very special, no roast beef or anything, I couldn't afford it. The children played inside and were not allowed outside on a Sunday. Maybe they were sent for a walk – maybe to the Botanics. I didn't go, I never had the time."

A Sunday outing to Inverleith Park. Date unknown.

"I went to the church a lot – I was very churchy. My mum wasn't as churchy as me then but she got more into it as she got older. She wouldn't miss a Sunday. The children went to Sunday School. Ian came home one day and said 'Mr McPherson (the superintendent) says we've to send our old gloves to somewhere'. And I said 'What would they be wanting old gloves for?' and it dawned on me, it was to send 'our love'!"

"We went to Stockbridge Church and Sunday School every Sunday. In fact, since I was a toddler. You got a sweetie to keep you quiet. I used to sit on my mother's knee and I've still got her locket with my teeth marks in it from biting it in the church. I went to Sunday School from age four right through to being a teacher myself. We used to go up to the General Assembly from the church. We had to walk all the way up there and back.

On the first Sunday they had all the Sunday Schools for a special service. The church was very important then, it was a lot of our social life. In our church we were in the children's choir and we used to have concerts. We all dressed up and wore our mother's old clothes and all the old fashioned things. Some people had some fantastic clothes – like the Laird of Cockpen. Our mothers all helped, they were interested in what we were doing. If you missed the church, the minister came round to see why you weren't there. You'd see him coming and run to your mother and tell her 'The minister's coming!' and you'd run out again."

"My father was the greatest one for taking us away in the car on a Sunday. We had a caravan at Thorntonloch and we used to go to Kenmore or Dunbar. He wouldn't take anyone else with him. He said it would be bad enough if anything happened to his own when he had them out. We went out as a family. We had a row about putting out washing on a Sunday. That was something no-one was allowed to do. Even if you had a baby. Connie did my washing once and hung it out and Nanny J and Mrs H and my mother had a row about it. Of course, that was a main street across to the park (Bell Place) and people came down that street to go for walks. You just couldn't do it."

"After Sunday School you had to take your clothes off then sit in the house, unless your mother took you out to visit friends in Musselburgh. You weren't allowed to play in the street. You had to go to your bed at six o'clock in the summer time – it was murder. Other kids in the street playing and you couldn't get to sleep for them playing. She was strict that way."

"We always went to church and to Sunday School after. I still go, I'm the only one left in the family now, and I still go to the Dean. At Sunday School we read passages from the Bible, in turn, each in the class, and then we'd talk about it. This was with everybody in your age group, girls, boys separate, and a teacher, in a little group together. And finish up with a hymn and a prayer all together. We used to have the Sunday School picnic in the summer, and the party at Christmas. At the picnic you got a bag and you took your own cup or whatever. You made tea for the adults and you ran races, had sports. And that was a great day's outing. And the Christmas party was lovely with all sorts of games and that. It was held in the church hall. They had party games for the children; the Grand Old Duke of York and all the usual, and Santa usually came with a little gift which was something. We were delighted with anything we got."

A kinderspiel at Saint Stephen's Church.

"We went to Saint Stephen's Church. In those days all the kids went to Sunday School. It was the done thing and nearly all the kids were from Stockbridge. Saint Stephen's used to put on kinderspiels. That Mr Yuil used to do it. He was a senior elder and a senior Sunday School teacher and a lawyer. When the kids went to church it didn't matter what was happening in the church if a kid was making a row he just used to walk round and along the corridor and give them a good clip across the ear and then go back to his seat again. Sunday School was the big thing. They had a big procession once a year up to the Waverley Station to get the train to Pinkiehill in Musselburgh. Everyone had a new shiny tinnie and a bit of white tape for the Sunday School picnic."

"You had to wear your Sunday-go-to-meeting clothes on Sundays and you got a proper breakfast then. Sausage and egg, or maybe a bit of bacon. And then we had a kind of dinner/tea. We often had fish or something special, but we didn't have dinner and tea. Probably a jeely piece in between. We weren't really allowed to play on a Sunday in the street. We went to the cemetery or maybe your uncle would come and take you out, or we went to the Botanical Gardens. We often went down to Granton – to the yacht when it was our turn."

"We went to Saint Mary's Cathedral. We still do. On Sundays you went to church in the morning, sometimes in the evening. You weren't allowed to go out and play in the streets. At that time, you weren't supposed to walk up the road whistling on a Sunday. That sort of thing was frowned on."

"We used to go to Dean Street Church – it was made into a picture house – and opposite it was the Sunday School. It's still got the name up I think – Dean Street Church Hall. When the church closed we were joined on to Saint Bernard's in Henderson Row. Well it was Mr Moir that was the minister, and he didn't allow any entertainment of any kind. No picnics for the children, no soirées, no concerts. A girl I was friendly with was a member of Saint Stephen's so I said to mother 'I'm going to join' and then the family gradually followed."

"We went to the Wesley Hall Sunday School which is now the theatre in Hamilton Place. We loved that. They had concerts every year. We got prizes. We did an exam on the Bible. Went to the Girl Guides, the Brownies – and the Salvation Army. We didn't get out if we didn't go somewhere!
  We really belonged to the Queen Street Church and I still go to that. Its amalgamated with the one on George Street – Saint Andrews. They were very ...all toffs you know. You had to be awful well behaved. There was a Mr Brown Douglas and he lived in Moray Place. He was a bachelor and his sisters never got married. And he used to have our Sunday School party. We were in the Bible class then and he took the Bible class. Beautiful house, four flats and all the great big beautiful gold-framed pictures and everything of the best. We thought this was marvellous. We had some fun. It was mixed boys and girls.

At the picnics we ran all the races, we were good runners and we used to get a lot of prizes. And your tinny round your neck, carried on a tape. You took your own money for you tea. We used to go right at the top of Arboretum Avenue. That used to be a big field called the 'Daisy Park'. We had quite a lot of Sunday School picnics there. There were ball games and races. We used to go on a train to Corstorphine – is it Pinkiehill? There was tunnels and it was dark when you went through, so of course there were high jinks in the tunnels.

Sundays you got up and had your bacon and egg and went away to the Wesley Hall about half past 12. Then we came back. We must have had soup or something. We always had roast beef on a Sunday or steak pie at about 4.30. My mother made home-made steak pies. You always had a pudding of some kind. We were in Sunday School in the afternoon. We mostly stayed in on a Sunday night. I had a big doll and it was locked away in a box my father had and it was locked away till next Sunday. It was kept perfect. You got to walk around the street with this doll. You were never allowed to have it during the week. And your Sunday clothes were folded away. Sunday shoes. We could pass them down."

"On Sunday morning you got up and had your breakfast, you maybe had a long lie. Then you went to Sunday School and my mother didn't make lunch on a Sunday. We had what we called a tea-dinner about 4ish. And then maybe sandwiches for your supper about nine. And then when you got older you left the Sunday School and you went to the Bible class. Our church had what was called the Guild of Youth. And there were a lot of the young ones and they had meetings and social occasions at night. They had the badminton and a dramatic society which I was a member of. I wasn't a very good one I don't think.

You never hang washing out on a Sunday. There was an awful stramash – it was after the war and Miss Yeaman was a tenant in the house opposite. My mother was away on holiday and we were having friends of Billy's from Holland and this was well after the war. I don't think my mother had extra curtains or bedspreads, and I washed them for the beds up the stair where the couple were going to sleep. And I hung them out on a Sunday because I was working and Miss Yeaman just about went past herself, so I wrote and told my mother – she was in Aberdeen. I said 'Mum, I hung the washing out on a Sunday in the garden and Miss Yeaman wasn't pleased'. My mother came home on the Saturday, she always brought some fish home from the market, she always gave Miss Yeaman a bit. She just took it over, and she wasn't right in the door before...'Helen had washing out on Sunday.'...and my mother said 'Yes, I know, and I was very pleased it was all ready done for me coming home'. That were her gas in a peep. And that was the attitude it was. Oh you never went out to play on a Sunday. You went a walk but you never went out to play."

Changed times – Colonies children playing in the street on a Sunday in the 1970s.

Shops, shopping and local services

"I used the Store and Linton's. I went to the Store for practically everything because I got my dividend for it. There was Nellie Robertson in Bridge Place, she had the dairy. I didn't get my milk from Nellie's, I got it delivered by the Store. We just paid tokens. I got things occasionally from Nellie's. There was a dressmaker and a man who was lame, he had the sweetie shop, the last shop on the block. He was a nice old man – the children often went there for sweeties. The coalman came round twice a week. Eighteen pence a bag. 'Coal, coal, coal' he used to call. Brotchie was his name. A vegetable cart used to come sometimes."

"We used the Store mostly – I felt it was just like going to a supermarket – everything was there when you got your weekly messages and it was more reasonable that the wee shops, although we used Linton's sometimes. There was Laidlaw's, the sweetie shop; and the McKendrick's had a fruit and vegetable shop, and there was a bicycle shop and Nellie the dairy. I used that quite a lot, and then the dressmakers came later."

"We'd go mainly to the Store but we shopped in Raeburn Place too. The pub at the corner of Raeburn Place has always been there. People used to go there for beer in a jug to take home. Granny Kinnear from our street used to do that, she'd go in the side door, she was a great character.

We used the shop along the Colonies too. That was Harvey's. He always had his grocer's apron on – a real grocer, he was very good. We would get a pennyworth of this and a pennyworth of that, you know, my mother would send me along. There was Mr Laidlaw's sweetie shop. We'd press our noses on the window and say 'Now, we'll get so many of this and so many of that'. The selection was fantastic, you couldn't decide – licorice stick, cinnamon sticks, you name it, he had it.

The McKendricks had a wee fruit shop. There was Nellie, the dairy. We'd go in there too and spend our money. We got milk there too but we mainly got our milk delivered from Grieve in Deanhaugh Street. If we ran short we got it from Nellie. Then there was the dressmaker. She was a friend of the Kelly's who stayed in Dunrobin Place. I sometimes used to get things made there. There were two sisters – one was a better dressmaker than the other – well, I thought so anyway.

Mackenzie in Cumberland Street, he brought the coal, and there was Johnny the fishman, and Rizzi the ice-cream man. The butcher came round for your order in the morning at 8 o'clock and delivered it later at 11 o'clock. We had Adamson, the sweep, twice a year."

"We used to go through the park to Wilson's the butcher at Canonmills, and the dairy, Burns – he used to deliver the milk and we'd pay it on a Saturday. We went to McDonald's for the paper. We went to Nellie's if we needed extra or Linton's for bits and pieces. Mother used the Store at Canonmills."

"There was Harvey's and then it was Elmslie's, then Linton and Kelly. It's changed hands a lot. I think we just used that shop sometimes. She went to the Store in Hamilton Place. You got everything in the Store. Then we'd go to the Maypole in Haugh Street and get eggs and stuff. We'd get bread and buns and biscuits – mixed biscuits broken. There was Thomson's the bicycle shop. They moved to Brandon Terrace. You could hire a bike for 6d an hour.

Elmslie's shop (now The Colony Shop).

We got the milk ourselves. We used to have cans with handles on. In fact the whole lot of us used to run messages for Nellie. We used to go to 'Cattie Annie's' where the new houses in Saint Bernard's Row are – across from there.

I remember a man came round with a dancing bear and a man came round with your milk – 'the soor milk cart'. We called it soor-dook. My mother used it for baking and we used to drink it too. Jimmy Rizzi, the ice-cream man, oh he was a great lad. His son was in Dean Street and his father came round with the cart and his brother used to play the fiddle and then he was the one-man band in Princes Street. I mind the rag and bone man too, with balloons. My mother used to get dishes from a woman for rags, or buy them, and then we'd go and break them.

The sweep was Corrie in India Place. He fell off the roof and broke his leg and he was up on the roofs with his leg in a stookie. He took a good drink. They took a good drink in those days!"

"Linton's had the shop on the corner, run by a man, his son and daughter. They worked all hours of the clock, nothing too much trouble, and they delivered goods, not like today when we have to carry everything. He was known all over for his very fine boiled ham. The dairy and the bakery and Bridge Place were handy too. The bakery sold delicious home-made baked scones. Of course there were quite a few deliveries – post, bread, milk and a fish van came from Canonmills. There was a lady at Number 1 or 2 Reid Terrace who did sewing. We had a weekly horse-drawn collection of refuse, but people had to supply their own buckets."

"Nellie Robertson had the dairy but mother had a pot delivered one day and it was green round the .... and the green was in the pitcher lid and that was that. Then the Dumfriesshire began to deliver milk in glass bottles. I remember going to Nellie's and I never saw the cat and the cat made a claw at me and I've been frightened of cats ever since.

Laidlaw's sweetie shop was always packed on a Saturday night with folk getting sweeties. My dad used to buy a bo-peep chocolate every week. Johnny the Fish came down. It was too much going up and down the streets, and he stood at the end of Glenogle Road. But the fish came right from Newhaven. He came for years. For 6d you got half-a-dozen herring, one shilling or 1/6d for haddock and tail of cod was about 6d. But then my dad only earned £3 a week."

"The dairy was a great place to go and get all the news. The centre of the universe – if you wanted any news you got it from there. You took your jug or whatever along and got it measured out. They lived at the back so she'd to go along a big passage to the back and the door made a big ring when you opened it, so that she could hear it if she was out the back. And the last house, it's always been like that the way it is, I've never known that window to have anything dressed as a shop, it was someone who did sewing who was in it, when we were younger. Dressmaking and alterations.

I don't remember newspapers funnily enough. I can remember the magazines. Schoolgirl's Own – I could hardly wait for the next week for it coming out, when you could read the rest of the story."

The Bridge Place shops as they were in about 1902.

"No. 1 wasn't a shop, No. 2 was that Miss Graham who was a seamstress. No. 3 that was Nellie Robertson's the dairy, then coming along to Mrs McKendrick's house. Then there was Miss Cullen (No. 5). My lads called her the kiddiejoylady because she sold them lollipops. She didn't open all the time. That's a house now. After Miss Cullen it was Jack, then Mrs Viddler. After Mrs Viddler it was us (Goodall's). We took over in 1970. Unfortunately, my wife took a heart attack in '74 and at that time I was an inspector on the buses and I had to do early shift, night shift...it just wasn't working and we sold it. We sold it to Abdul. He leased it. There were two people after that.

Then there was Kelly's shop. When we came down here first, it was Mr Linton. He stayed somewhere in the Newington area. You used to see him coming down at 10 o'clock in the morning ...'Good morning, good morning'...to the shop. His assistant whose name was John, well of course John would have been there from 8 o'clock in the morning. In these days of course they patted the butter up and cut the cheese with wire – a proper grocer's shop it was. Jim Kelly came after. He was there 25 years so he probably came say 1962 and it's changed hands three times since then."

"If you went up to the Store you sat on a form and got talking to everyone. You waited for your turn. They bagged everything for you. Whatever you were buying came loose and they bagged up a pound or a quarter or whatever you wanted. The shop here was run by Mr Linton. He used to boil his own ham and if you went along with a jug he'd give you the stock. It was a nice shop. They used to bottle up beer in those days."

"Harvey – he didn't always clear out empty boxes but used to wait till the bonfire came along and then a swarm of kids used to descend like locusts and clear the place out. I remember my uncle saying when Linton was there that all the old worthies that like a dram...you'd go in the shop and you went round the back and you got a glass. He wasn't supposed to sell it that way but I think it was always done. I think the law was a bit easy-ozy then. Rizzi, the Italian ice-cream man with his wee horse and his fancy cart, came once a week. He didn't speak that good English but he had a beautiful little pony."

"The Store had everything – butcher, fishmonger, grocer, chemist, baker, drapery, shoes, wallpaper too. When it was the divi time we all got something special. That was twice a year. That's why we used the Store. We went to the Buttercup and Lipton's too. We got our shopping delivered every week by the horse-drawn van. Brownlee, the butcher, delivered too. Stamford's were our milk people. We got it delivered in a pitcher and we had to put the empty one out. Sometimes we had to go with our pitcher to the top of the street. That might have been in wartime. He had a cart and an Airedale dog."

"Mother never carried any messages. The butcher used to come for the orders and the grocer's wife used to come too. I remember her, she had a long ear trumpet and she came in and had a long blether with mother then took the order. And then a message boy brought the orders down. The baker came round. Our grocer was in Dean Bank Terrace. My mother was never a member of the Store. She got the bread there in the war – she thought it was nice bread, better than you'd get from the shops. If we wanted anything extra we used the local shop."

"The dairy didn't have an awful lot of sweets. She sold milk and then there was that place up the pend which had cows and everything – Ramage – where the Savoy cinema was. They had cows and we went there with a pitcher for milk – and a drink on the way back! The dairy had big cans of milk and these things used to hang on that you measured the milk out with. Lovely and fresh.

Laidlaw had a really lovely shop. It had every kind of sweetie you could think of and they kept newspapers and comics. And an old-fashioned thing with a lid with all kinds of biscuits at the side of the counter. And he kept it perfect. In the window there was every bottle of every kind of sweetie you could think of. Mind you, so did the dairy sell sweets. These bars of toffee. We used to get a penny to go to the pictures on a Saturday afternoon and a penny to spend and we used to stand at that shop window and get half a bar of treacle toffee or half a bar of lemonade toffee and we used to sit and suck that in the picture house."

"There was a fruit man – Gordan. When he retired there was a man going to buy his business but he backed out because he was going to have to get up too early in the morning ! And Gordan had a good business and used to come down the street, and oh, there was a queue. But he could only go the length of I think the middle street. He started at the first street, at the Canonmills end, and he came along, but be couldn't go any further than the middle street because of the shop – Linton's. He must have had to go just so far."

Jocky Hogg and Mr Graham on their fruit and
vegetable cart, pulled by Hopey the horse.
They delivered produce to the Colonies.

Games and play

"The children didn't play in the river or the Bell's Park much – more Inverleith Park or the pond. Finlay fell in the pond twice and was brought home on the Store milk cart. There was a Parkie who opened and closed the gates of the Bell's Park every day at dawn and dusk – he used to chase the kids if they were playing there."

"We used to play 'dodge'. You had sides and you shouted your numbers and then you threw a ball at them – something like rounders. Skipping ropes, French ropes. Our mothers and fathers used to come out to play with us. They'd come out and hold the skipping ropes for us, play rounders, or dodgy with us. Not just our family, it was a right wee community down here. We played football in the street and watched for Adizet coming. We used to shout 'shot!' when we saw him. Hares and hounds. Right round Inverleith Terrace and back home again. We played in Inverleith Park on the swings. We also played a lot on the Dumby Steps. We played at schools up there and slid down the banisters to see who'd get down the bottom first. One would come down the stairs and one down the banisters. We'd be doing somersaults down the banisters too. We had very little, but we didn't need it.

There were seasons for skipping ropes, peevers, bowls, peeries and diablo, scrap collecting, and in the summer Peggy Hill used to teach us crochet. We'd sit in the garden and do that. It was scorching. Sometimes we had wee concerts and charged a halfpenny or a penny to come and watch. We'd dress up and do our turns. We had roller skates and when Inverleith Pond was frozen the Reid's had ice skates and we'd get a shot of them. When we had snow, we'd build a fort at the bottom of the street and have snow fights. They'd come from other streets and VOOM!"

"We played in the street if we got peace from Mrs Mackie. She lived in Bell Place but her window looked on to the street and if you were making a noise she was always knocking on the windows! She'd say 'Get across to the Park,' and if you went the parkie used to chase you!"

"We were never away from the river. Fishing for Beardies and all those kinds. The parkies or baillies never bothered you unless you were doing damage. We used to go to the Park to play football, and to the pond. We used to have a Mr Kelly who had a lovely yacht up there. He used to race them up at the pond. It was great in those days; of course, it used to be a big pond and there was a big hut to keep the boats in. Mr Kelly and his two sons Jimmy and Johnny they used to make rare yachts. I used to fish for minnows in jars and I used to play in the Bell's Park too, in among the trees."

"You tied a rope to the paling. The old lady in No. 21, she used to kick up because we were pulling her railing and she was raging because they were playing a game – we call it Cock O'Rosie. Somebody stood in the middle of the street to try to catch you and you had to run from one pavement across to the other. Well of course when they came back they were dodging and they slammed into the paling and she was out raging at them and shaking her stick at them. I heard my mother at the door and we always remember that she said 'I've just told her the laddies that were hanging the paling a few years ago, they're in France fighting to keep you safe in your bed, so go in and make yourself a cup o' tea."

Rocheid Path in the Bell's Park – a favourite place to play.

"There was quite a group of young people at that time and we played peevers – that's the chalk tables on the ground – and diablo, and the boys had the peeries with the whips that on the ground used to make different colours on the top of them when they spun. For diablo you had two pieces of wood with string between them and the diablo – like an egg timer almost but made of wood. It was much wider at the ends, but the middle came to about nothing and you had to balance that on the string and balancing it you threw it up in the air and caught it, on the piece of string, and it was just to see how many times in the air you could catch it. It was quite difficult to do.

When we stayed in Glenogle Terrace we would always be playing in the water because we were so close to it. We played a lot in Rocheid Park as there were bushes and there was great scope for hide and seek. While on the subject, my brother accidentally found a body there. It was as you go over the bridge and go left as if you were going towards the Park – it was playing that he found the body. He had committed suicide with a bottle of lysol. It created a bit of a stir.

But one of our favourite games in the winter was getting trays from my mother and going along the path in Rocheid Park where there was a slope down to the Water of Leith – there were railings of course – and when the snow was on the ground it was super, a super slide, we used to slide right down. I wouldn't like to tell you the state of the trays at the end. We couldn't afford sledges so that was the nearest we could get to the real ones."

"I can remember at this time of year when there were all these leaves we used to pile them up and make walls, make houses, play at houses us girls. Oh aye, we played at kick-the-can at the top of the street, hide-and-seek, skipping ropes, oh that was a great favourite. I just remember going in a line and jumping two and going out, and the next one in... The boys I think were terribly wild, my two brothers were the wildest of the lot I think. They used to say, that's just like the thing, the policeman's sons being the wildest."

"We played the bowls, cuddies loups – one would lean against the garden paling and bend down and others would jump on top and when one fell off he joined on the one that was bending down and it eventually all collapsed; battleships – you took the name of a battleship and there was one on either side of the street and you just whipped and dug each other; then statues and peevers. Then Bella McBain, she was good at diablo – the only one in the Colonies who could do it. Then there was kick-the-can and allevoi. They were popular ones as well. 'Cat and bat'– you played with a little bit of wood and it had 1, 2, 3, 4 on it and it had pointed ends and you hit the bevelled end and then gave it a clatter with the bat, so it was a sort of cricket-come-rounders. And fire-cans, that had a craze for a while. You'd get an old syrup tin, get two holes in it and put wire as a handle then you put paper and sticks and sometimes a bit coal in it and you lit it and you hurled it round and round till it was red hot, and that was it.

The Water of Leith was used by practically all of the Colonies kids; they lived in that place in the summer time. Occasionally you got chased by the water baillie or the police but it was half-hearted; they went through the motions and you pretended to go away. There wasn't any fishing then."

"I don't remember the Water of Leith being as dirty then as it has been in recent years. There were fish in it. I was one of a crowd who used to go down to the Watt's house at the end of this street. The second son, Alec, was a great one for standing perfectly still in the water with a spade, waiting for a trout to come. He did occasionally succeed in catching one. I never tried it. There were people who used to fish with rods and lines.

We played kick-the-can. Someone used to kick the can as far as they could and all the rest ran away and hid and one person retrieved the can. It was like hide-and-seek really. This was one of the games we used to play on the main road. I suppose it originated because kids couldn't afford a ball so they used anything they could.

The girls would play peevers on the pavement. Of course we used to invade their privacy sometimes. But they had diablos. The boys had peeries and whips at certain times of year. We didn't play them all the time. It was like chestnuts, just played at one time of year."

"We used to make tents out of old blankets and carpet on the pavement. You put sticks in the cobbles and tied strings on an old blanket. Another thing we did was play with scraps. We played that a lot. We sat on the stairs and changed scraps. Pictures of angels and so on. It's a thing you never see now. We use to get an old Woodbine box from Linton's or the sweetie shop, and we used to keep all our scraps in there. We traded them. If you got a big angel and you were changing it, well they had to give you enough scraps to cover the big one.

I used to sit and crochet all these balls of coloured wool. We used to go and buy them with our pocket money and sit on the steps and crochet. We were easy pleased in these days, eh? We used to play in the Bell's Park. We used to run home and get our pieces and jam and a pitcher of tea and go back and have a picnic. We played among the bushes and slid down the hills. We took dolls and played houses. We used to fish up the pond in the Park but not in the river."

School

"In my day, lots of boys I was pally with went to Heriot Watt and they got a great education free but they had to get the marks to get there, and then they got good jobs in Bruce Peebles and places as engineers. They made their own way because they were interested."

Pupils at Stockbridge School, Hamilton Place. Taken in 1945.

"At Stockbridge School it was the three Rs as my father would say. We had lots of games as well. We had overball, netball, but basically the three Rs. There was no music teacher or any foreign language or anything like that and when the war started we were actually put into a room in the Salvation Army and they closed the school. Uniform wasn't compulsory but you were expected to wear a gym dress, which I did, and black stockings – anyone who could afford it. We were punished by the belt and didn't get out of school into the community."

"I went to Stockbridge Primary for about three years and then I went to Heriot's where I had to pay. If you didn't go to a Merchant Company school and didn't do so well you went to Bellevue (now Drummond High). My sister went to Broughton as they went up to fifth year. Stockbridge School had a black cap with about half-a-dozen yellow stripes round it and the badge was a glorified 'S' for Stockbridge. At Broughton School you weren't allowed at school if you didn't wear a uniform. The only time you were out of Stockbridge School was sports day."

"I started at Hamilton Place, then I went to Trinity Academy for Secondary. I couldn't get in to Broughton. Trinity was a very good school. It was near Newhaven Station and we could get the train to school. It was really something to do that. We often cycled to Trinity and sometimes we cycled to Craigleith Station for the sake of going on the train to Trinity. It was very posh, you know, a train to school. When I went to Trinity I think they paid about ten shillings. I don't know whether that was a term or a year. My sisters went to Broughton– that wasn't fee paying."

"The year we came down here, I went to Holy Cross Academy in Ferry Road. It's no longer there of course. I took a tram from Brandon Terrace up to Golden Acre then you transferred over to another tram. We used to get a transfer ticket. Holy Cross was down towards Leith. I didn't come home for lunch."

"I went to Stockbridge School then to Broughton. You had to be an 'A' pupil to go to Broughton otherwise you went to Flora Stevenson's. When we went it was ten shillings a year. I remember on the morning we had to take our money I asked my father for the money – he kept the money. Three of us went there. The others always said they didn't want to go to Broughton. I don't know whether they got As or not but they didn't want Latin, French and science and things that we got. I liked the school."

"We all started at Stockbridge School. When you left after what they called 'the qualifying' you went to the Secondary School. Sally went to Broughton and I was going there but the day before the holidays we were told that everywhere was full so I had to go to another school, and you'd to choose it quickly. Well, all the other girls were going to Boroughmuir so I went there. It was ten shillings a year. That was a lot of money."

Outings and leisure

"I took the children around a lot – to the Park – to Port Seton nearly every Sunday. Ally used to cycle and when the boys were able they'd cycle too and Helena and I would go by bus."

"I was a member of the Girl's Auxiliary. We went out on excursions. We would go up to the Pentlands or out to pick primroses near Blackshiels. We'd pick the flowers and troop back to get the bus home. That was on a Saturday afternoon.

We had a happy time, it was a good place to be a child in. You got a penny on a Saturday but you were happy with it. Sometimes you got a penny to go to the Savoy with. My husband used to take a jeelie jar to get into the pictures. I remember people taking jam jars for the Savoy and the Grand, not the Ritz, they were a wee bit more posh. We mostly went to the Savoy and the Pavilion, that was up Dean Street, where the big archway is."

Travelling 'up town' was done on foot, or on a tram like the one shown here at the tram terminus at Comely Bank (taken around 1916).

"Wednesday night, we both went out to the Empire or the Rutland. Saturdays we went shopping. We would go to PTs for high tea or to Tollcross, Blythes or the Brown Derby in Frederick Street. Sometime we would play whist on a Friday at the Savoy. George would go for a pint on a Saturday."

"My dad worked hard all his life and he maybe used to go for a pint when he'd finished work – maybe 8.30-9 o'clock at night. He used to go to the Territorial Arms (the Terry's) and he was also a member of the Royal Engineers Club and that's where he went on a Saturday night and met his pals. My mother sewed. In later life she went to the PTA. We went to Mrs Howieson's in Clarence street, dancing, and my mother made the costumes and our clothes. We used to go round the hospitals and give concerts. We went to Parker's Store in Bristo Street and got one-shilling-a-yard material to make them."

"I went to the Savoy cinema. They used to have billiards up above too. There used to be two old women, sisters from Barnton Terrace, one used to play the fiddle and one the piano. You used to have to stretch you neck to see the film for them playing away. It was funny, so it was."

"We always had a lot of books about. We played board games together in the house, and card games. There was the snakes and ladders and the draughts, and my father loved dominoes, and he was always needing someone to play dominoes. We got one brother who was a bit of a comedian and he used to make us all laugh pretending he was the Minister!"

"Both my parents had bikes. They would take a run out to Crammond. We had a holiday house over in Fife and this house here was handy for the boat. Every week-end when we could, we got things packed up and went over there from Granton. I think the boat went twice a day. I remember running down on the pier to catch the boat. We caught the tram down to Granton from Canonmills."

"We used to go to a dance hall in Pitt Street – Saint Bernard's Hall – on a Saturday morning. You got an hour-and-a-half old-time dancing and an hour-and-a-half Highland dancing. No band. That was just all school children. There was a picture house up Dean Street and another one, the Savoy, in Saint Bernard's Row. And the one in Dean Street – children in arms were admitted free so I used to carry my youngest brother in when he was about as big as me and my sister used to get tickets and then we could spend his penny. My father always used to have a bath on a Saturday afternoon so we were all sent out."

"We went to the pictures. To the Savoy and the Grand. There was the Pavilion in Dean Street where the National Trust place is. Then there was the Ritz opposite Heriot Hill. It was a beautiful picture house. Then the Grand – my mother minded that they had a circus in it. We used to go to the Savoy on a Saturday for a matinée, or the Grand. There was a place down Leith Walk, the Alhambra, and sometimes they had a kind of theatre. As a treat you got taken down there.

Then there was the Theatre Royal and Sally and I at Christmas used to go and queue to get in, and your mother would give you shortbread and current loaf and an apple or orange to eat in the queue because you might be an hour in the queue so's you could get in the front row. The Theatre Royal burnt down. It was a nice theatre, we used to get some good things there. We had a wireless, I mind because my father got one of those crystal sets and built it. And then we got another one. But you didn't have all the things that the kids have now to play with. I mean you made your own amusements, maybe jigsaw puzzles or something like that, but it was mainly reading – we all read."

Three generations of the Fyfe family, taken in 1885.

Annual events and special occasions

Bonfires

"We had bonfires – one at Bell Place and one opposite Linton's. The boys used to have fights – pinch each other's stuff. Between the two of them there was just a running battle all the time. They used to put tatties in and they'd come out black and still raw because they could never wait to leave them in long enough. They'd eat them anyway."

"On the bonfire day we used to have a great time. We'd have these balls on a rope and we'd birl it round about and batter people on the heid with it. We'd say 'Stop where you are. Are you Scotch or Irish?' and if you moved, you got battered. They were supposed to be made of paper, but some people put tatties in them. Our bonfire was at the top of the street and we used to pinch each other's bonfires, and we used to pinch from Stockbridge too."

"We had great fun at the bonfires. All the families were out. And there was a family came to stay at the bottom of out street – he was a policeman and his son was a policeman. They were all big people, and one of the boys, Charlie, I remember at the bonfire, put on one of these firework things and he blew off part of his finger. And of course we were in an awful state, we had to go way up the Infirmary to get his finger seen to."

"When you had bonfires, they had one and you had one – the other end – it was like two different places. The middle would be low doors of Balmoral. Our bonfire was at the top of the first street. Oh, it was an occasion. It was always at Queen Victoria's birthday, the 24th of May, and the bonfire was usually on the Monday. You had a holiday from school and you went collecting from all the houses, then the other end would come along the water and pinch all your bonfire stuff. The rows that went on! You sometimes stored it down by the Water of Leith. And then of course they came along the water and nicked it all. And some of them were really big boys, you didn't have a chance! I remember we went as far away as Eildon Street and dragged it all the way back through the short cut at the other end. My mother used to say 'Oh, you're filthy'.

You had this bonfire and you had squibs. And there was a boy lived in the next street, a boy Henderson, and he was lighting this firework and it wasn't lit properly and it blew up. I was standing next to him, and it blew his finger off. There wasn't many accidents. There was no November the Fifth fireworks then. It was only since all you English people came that we get November the Fifth! You just saved up your pennies to get fireworks. I got sparklers, I wasn't very ambitious. I was kind of frightened of them. The bonfire was in the street, the traffic had to go round it. Some had to turn back and go the other road."

Street parties

"We had just the one party for VE Day. Every street did their bit and the children were all in one street for their tea."

"I remember street parties at the end of the summer. The children would have their tea and in the evening we'd be waltzing in the street. Mrs Renton would have the teas in her house, and we'd have the bar in ours."

A VE Day street party in Kemp/Bell.

Tucking in at a VE Day street party.

"Oh, I can remember when at the time of the Coronation there were tables and forms right down the street. We had tea, cakes, sandwiches. There were flags from my window across to Mary's. A rope with little flags on."

"The street parties started during the war to raise money for buying things to send to the forces and they were 'to help win the war' sort of parties. Almost once a year."

"We only had parties when it was the war. At the end of the war. We got tables from the Baths. We had a party in our street. The low doors of Collins and the low doors of Colville and us. We had tables all the way down the street .... sandwiches and cakes. Everybody did something."

"We had street parties when the war was on. The 14-18 War – there was a family at the foot of Balmoral who were schoolteachers. O'Hennarchy was their name and they organised a concert. They had a tent and it was really good. They had all the songs, 'It's a long way to Tipperary'…and all those songs. They had community singing. I think it was a penny to go to those concerts. We had a party down our own street – Victoria party. Mrs Suttie was in the picture and the Suttie bairns and they were all with their fancy hats on."

A VE Day street party in Teviotdale/Dunrobin.

Wartime

"I'm a right anti-war person. I could have been arrested the way I was. I went up to the school to collect the gas masks. You've no idea how it felt. I had Helena in a long thing – she had to go in it if there was a gas attack, and you had to pump air into it. There was a Mickey Mouse one for Alisdair and another one for Ian. I said 'How am I supposed to do all this – get masks on and keep my feet going for the baby one?'

We didn't get evacuated. I had a friend near Bathgate and this house was vacant at the time. It was a right country cottage, dry closet and everything, but I loved it. We stayed there a year-and-a-half and we came back because I wasn't very well. I think it was the paraffin lamps. They were the old ones and they had a strong smell."

"They had a beautiful air raid shelter at Number 9 – with bus seats in red plush and once or twice she let the kids into the shelter to play. We didn't use the air raid shelter, we used the cupboard in the middle of the house. We had a big kist in it and we sat in there with our gas masks on. We had to squeeze in. It was rarely needed."

"During the First War the horses would come up along the top of the Colonies and right down to Leith to get on a boat and then they'd go to Belgium to get killed for horse meat for the people. That would be two or three times a week. They were big horses and they kept them in Veitch's Square and then walked them down to the docks. We all knew what they were going to."

"We were sent away in 1939 to Craigellachie in Banffshire. I have only happy memories of it, and the couple that took us in. I was with a girl from West Claremont Street, and we were together, and my mother went with my brother and she was up there for a year. She stayed with the school teacher. Then she had to come home because Granny took ill and we stayed up there. We were there for nearly three-and-a-half years."

"When the war finished everybody made for Princes Street. It was absolutely packed. You could hardly move in it with people singing and the jollification .... I mean there was no drinking, it was just everybody was high on the fact that the war had ended. Not quite so much on VJ Day when Japan surrendered, but more on VE Day."

"I worked through the war at Beaver's, but I was doing quite a bit of work for VAD. We went all over Britain. It took me around and about. We went down to London – to the bombs. I remember the first time we went down there. I'd been to London before, of course, but when I saw London, the houses and the streets!.... looking up at buildings which were just bits of rooms. It was hard the first time, but you got used to it. Oh I was scared, but I tried not to show it. Buzz bombs going over – sirens. We were sent to back up the services, to go round the shelters, the fire service, the underground stations and casualty at Saint Mary's Hospital."

"The people next door had an air raid shelter in the garden. I paid a few visits to that from time to time during air raids. You could get about eight people in them sitting down on benches along the side. They were dug down, you went down steps into them – they usually built turf on top.

I was still at school when the war started. You didn't attend school at first. It was all arranged that you went to different houses in the area – so many of you. We went to a house in Reid Terrace – the Smiths – until things got arranged for going back to school again. I didn't actually find out why, I think it just wasn't safe, and so many children in one building in case of air raids. I don't know if it was all children did it."

"In the war there were shelters along where the new insurance building is. When the siren went, if there was a bad one, we used to run along there. Fill the pram with stuff. There were some in the street as well. We used to go across to Number 1 Avondale. He had a wee room next to the road and they thought it was the safest. I used to take my two. We were all in the bed, her two and my two, and the men sitting. It was a squash, so many – so many at the top, so many at the bottom. You had your clothes on – you were just lying down."

"People next door to us had a shelter in their garden; certain people had them, but we didn't bother with one. Certain nights you were on duty and when the sirens went you had to race up to this air raid precautions place and stay there until the sirens went and then come back. You got training for first aid, and we also got trained for if there was gas. We'd wear these gas things. We actually did get into a room where there was gas. It was horrible. If someone had dropped a bomb here the casualties would probably be taken to Henderson Row, where the deaf and dumb school is. They had a full-time staff that were on during the day, but the volunteers went once a week and stayed there all night and slept in beds. Then you came home in the morning and you went to your work.

There was a bomb fell, up near the Park. Sally was coming along the road and she came beltin' home and it was somewhere quite close. And I think there was one round about Pilton, because the lady at the top of the street, and another lady opposite, they came to stay here after this bomb fell. Father was the air raid warden for these streets. I think there were two or three wardens in the Colonies. And certain people had stirrup pumps. If an incendiary fell, they had to get the pump out. I can't remember ever seeing anyone going into the air shelters."

An R101 over the Colonies in 1931 (seen above Dunrobin Place).

Changes in the neighbourhood

"There was no Snakey in those days. It was built when the wall at the steps fell down. They had to close the steps. I heard it fall down – what a racket. It was during the night. Somebody might have been killed if it hadn't been at night. It was the Academy side fell down.

   They still had gas light in the street. And the 'leerie'. The kids used to run after him calling 'leerie, leerie, light the lamp'."

"When the railings were taken away during the war, our neighbour gave them a backhander to get the railings left. We got ours from Craigleith quarry after the war where they'd been dumped."

"If you look at the river by the Falshaw Bridge, you'll see the wood where the boxings were. Long ago if the river ran dry they could used the boxes for water, to store it, or for fires. The water in the boxes was five feet deep. They're still there but they've been filled in with stones.

   They used to have water baillies who used to come round every week to see to all the stuff in the Water of Leith and take it away. There was an outlet from the Park, the pond there called the Skitterie Burn. It used to run through the Park."

"There used to be allotments where the Snakey is, three allotments. Mr Wilson and Mr Rutherford the postman, they had allotments. You weren't allowed on the Snakey in those days. Then they built steps at the side of the wall and then built the path when the wall fell down at the Dumby Steps. There was a gate in the wall and you had to have a key to get in to the allotments."

"We had a lamplighter at one time, oh yes, and we had to go in at once when he came because it was dark. He lit them with a long pole with a flickering thing at the top. He stuck it up from the bottom of the gas lamp to light it. It lifted the lid and turned on the jet. He came at dusk and he came round in the morning and put them out."

"The river was much cleaner, not as overgrown. We used to swim in it. The parkman used to come along and lock the gates at night. Even Bell Place was closed off. He used to come through at sunset shouting 'closing time'. There was a full-time park-keeper – about four of them – they had a hut by the pond. In the winter when it was frozen, they put lamps round for skating."

"There was a gas works along the other end of Glenogle Road, on the left-hand side, and there used to be a gasometer there, past the new houses. Glenogle Road had just the cossies (cobbles) then, as did most roads, but there was a stretch in front of the Edinburgh Academy on Henderson Row that was different. It was wooden bricks because they took away the noise, for it was horse and cart and all the wheels were metal shod, which made a lot of noise on the cossies."

"The gardens haven't changed much. We had a cherry tree and a rowan tree and that was taken down. I remember the doctor coming when Kelly had the fire, and he didn't know the place because the tree wasn't there. People objected to them."

"The Daisy Park – that was where Ramages used to have the cows. He was the farmer down in the pend behind the Savoy, and they had cows there – in cow sheds. He took the cows in the summer time up to the Daisy Park, where the playing fields are now at the top of Arboretum Avenue."

"The gardens haven't changed much". Mr and Mrs Alex Johnston and Mr William Douglas in the garden of 12 Rintoul Place in 1909.

"You were awfully well-off if you owned a bike. You used buses and trams, or you walked. Nothing ever came along Glenogle Road. You never thought anything of walking when you were children. When I went to Stockbridge School you were up and down those stairs all the time and that's how they called it the Dumby Stairs because the deaf and dumb children came down the stairs. I was quite old before I knew it was called Gabriel's Road. There was a notice up but the leaves had all fallen over it and when they took them away we thought, 'Oh, Gabriel's Road!'. And the deaf and dumb children went up one side and you went up the other side. It was just habit."

Arboretum Avenue – the road to the Daisy Park – taken at the turn of the century.